Sounds of
The Story of Musical Instruments

Chapter 1: The Grumpy Grand Piano

Chapter 2: The Power of Notes

Chapter 3: The Harmony Hotel

Chapter 4: The Magic of Together

Chapter 5: The Grand Performance

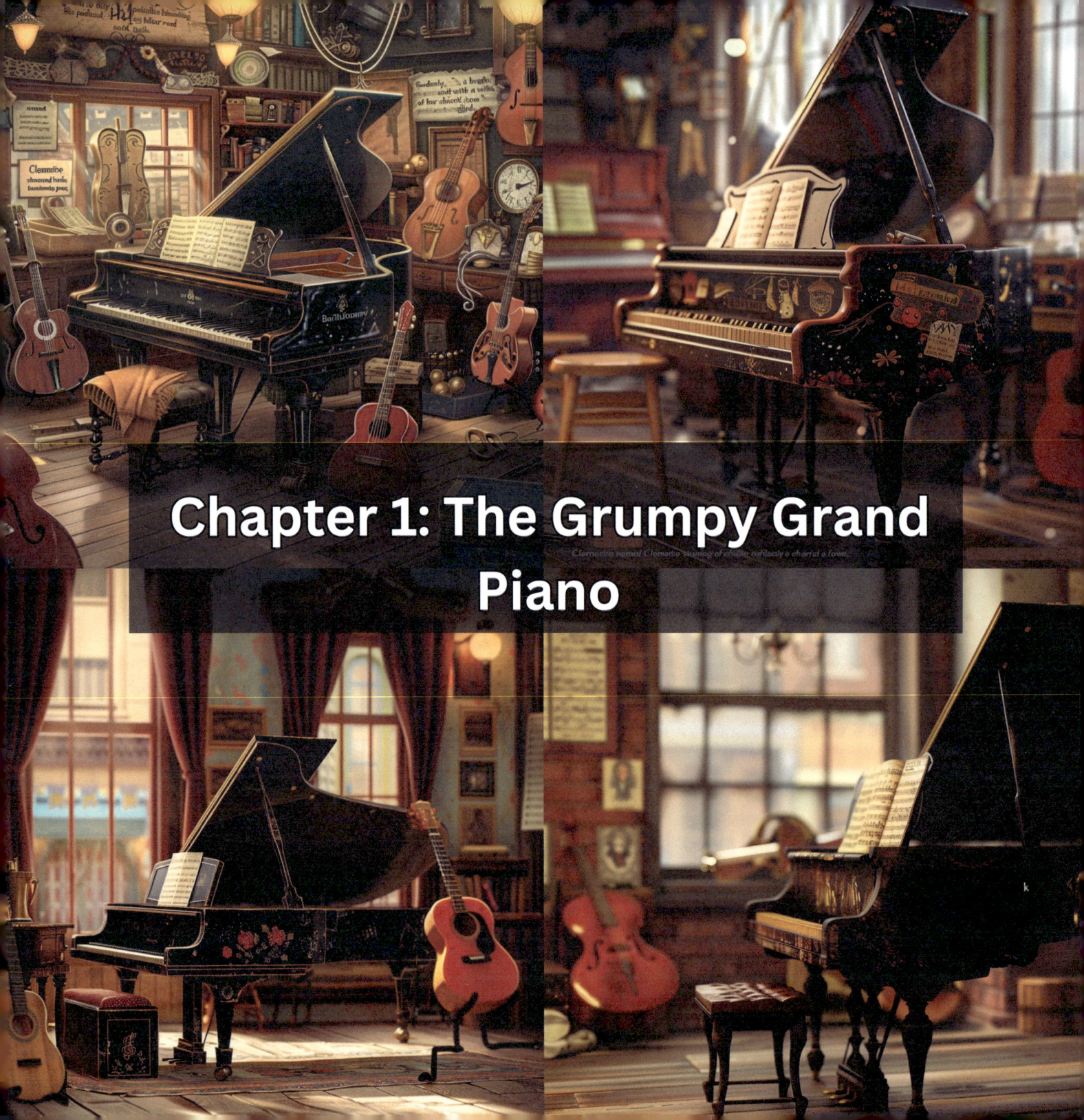

Chapter 1: The Grumpy Grand Piano

In the heart of Harmonyville, a grand piano named Bartholomew stood glumly in the corner of the music shop.

Unlike the other instruments, Bartholomew wasn't excited about finding a new home.

"Humph," he grumbled to himself, his polished black surface reflecting a frown.

"All these fancy fiddles and shiny trumpets get picked first. Who wants a dusty old piano like me?"

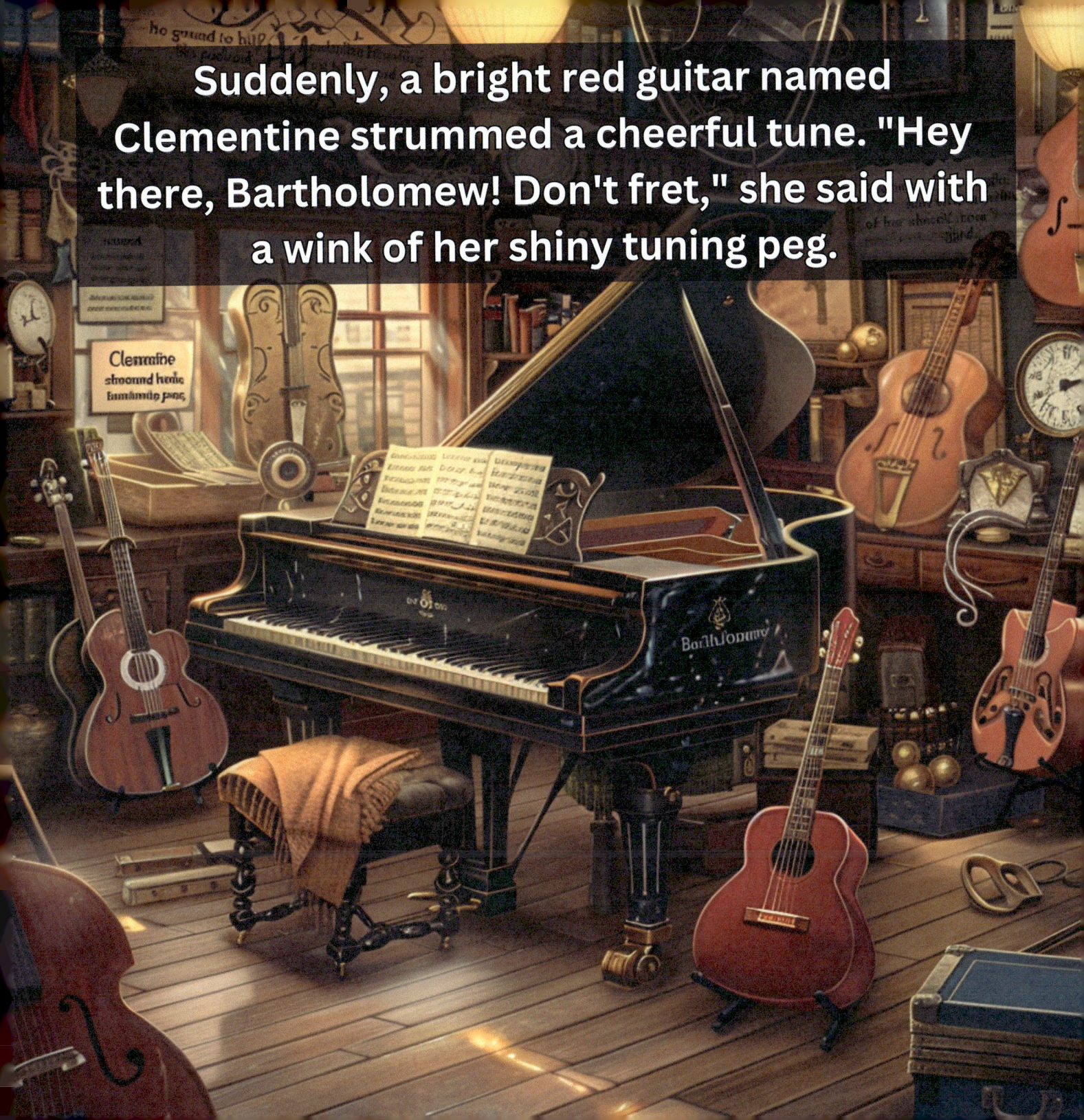

Suddenly, a bright red guitar named Clementine strummed a cheerful tune. "Hey there, Bartholomew! Don't fret," she said with a wink of her shiny tuning peg.

Bartholomew sighed. "Easy for you to say, Clementine. You're small and portable, perfect for campfire singalongs. I'm stuck here, too big for anyone to love."

Chapter 2: The Power of Notes

Clementine nudged Bartholomew with a string. "Don't you forget, my friend, we all have magic inside us.

We just need someone to play the right notes to unlock it!"

Bartholomew scoffed. "Magic? Notes? Sounds like silly talk."

Just then, a deep voice boomed from behind. "She's right, Bartholomew. We instruments hold the power to create something incredible – music!"

It was Bruno, the big, friendly bass guitar. His thick strings vibrated with a low hum.

"Music?" Bartholomew boomed, intrigued. "How can clanging keys or strumming strings be magical?"

Chapter 3: The Harmony Hotel

Bruno chuckled. "Imagine, Bartholomew, a place called the Harmony Hotel. Each of us is a guest, with our own special voice."

Clementine chimed in, "Bruno's deep notes are like the foundation of the hotel, strong and steady."

Bruno smiled. "And Clementine's bright melodies are like the sunshine streaming through the windows, making everyone happy."

Bartholomew's frown softened. "And what about me?"

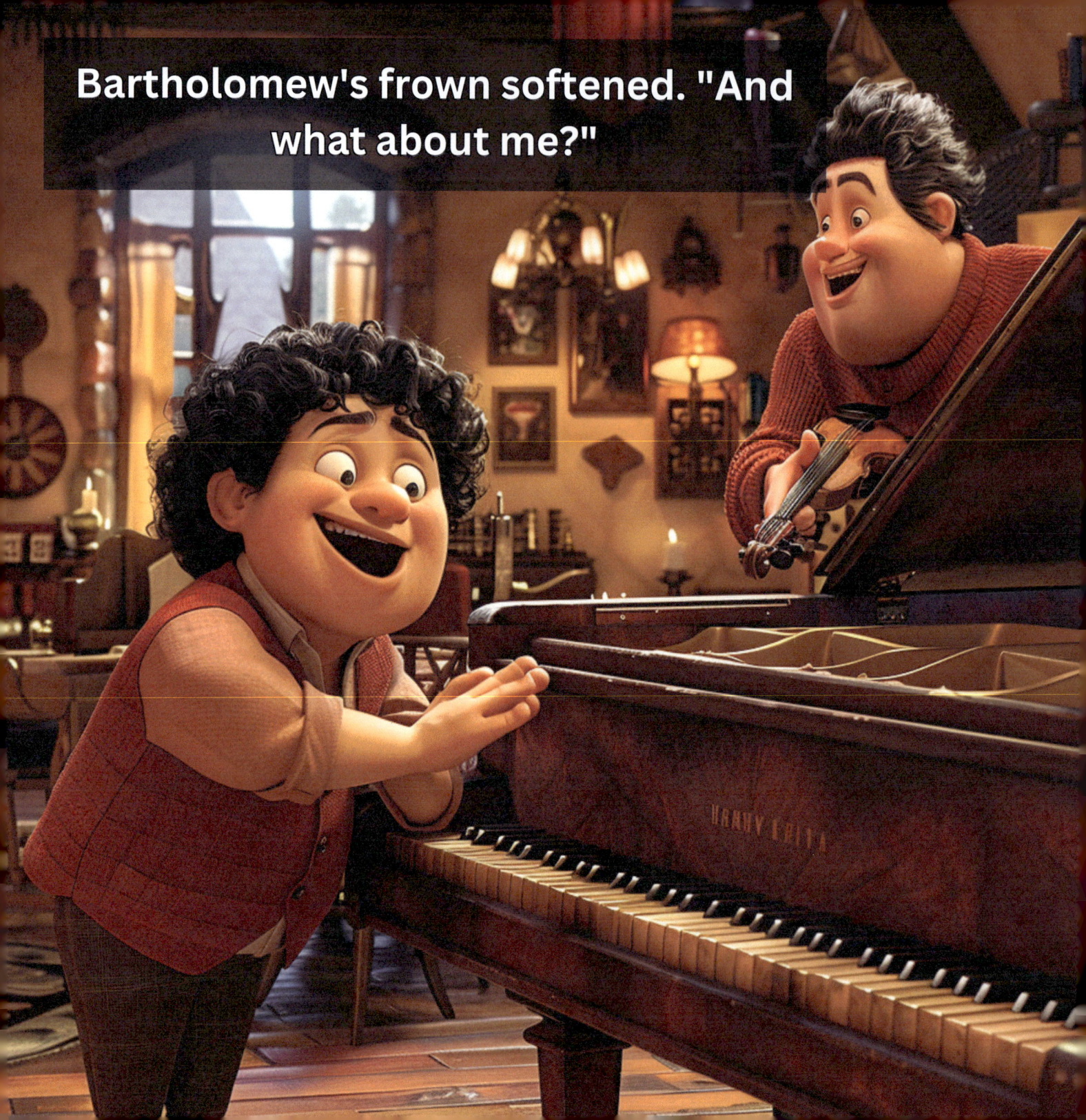

Chapter 4: The Magic of Together

"You, Bartholomew," Bruno said, "are the heart of the Harmony Hotel.

"Your deep notes can be soft whispers or grand pronouncements, setting the mood for the entire song."

Clementine strummed a playful tune. "But the real magic happens when we all play together!

> Imagine the melody dancing on your deep notes, Bruno, creating a beautiful harmony."

Bartholomew's keys twitched with excitement. He'd never thought of his music that way.

Chapter 5: The Grand Performance

Finally, a little girl named Lily skipped into the shop. Her eyes sparkled when she saw Bartholomew.

Her tiny fingers danced across his keys, coaxing out soft melodies that mingled with Clementine's playful strums and Bruno's deep bassline.

Lily giggled with delight. "This is beautiful! You sound amazing together!"

Bartholomew felt a warmth spread through his wooden frame. He wasn't just a dusty old piano;

he was part of something magical, something that made people happy.

From that day on, Bartholomew, Clementine, and Bruno all understood the power of music.

It wasn't about who was bigger or smaller, but about how their unique voices could blend together to create a symphony of joy.

They learned that true magic comes not from playing alone, but from playing in harmony.

Made in the USA
Columbia, SC
02 May 2025